Favorite Celtic Songs
for Easy Piano

Arranged by John Nicholas

Cherry Lane Music Company
Director of Publications/Project Editor: Mark Phillips
Project Coordinator: Rebecca Skidmore

ISBN 978-1-60378-097-1

Visit our website at www.cherrylaneprint.com

Contents

4 The Ash Grove

6 Believe Me, If All Those Endearing Young Charms

8 The Bluebells of Scotland

10 A Bunch of Thyme

18 Carrickfergus

12 Cockles and Mussels (Molly Malone)

14 The Croppy Boy

16 Danny Boy (Londonderry Air)

21 Eileen Oge

24 Finnegan's Wake

28 The Foggy Dew

27 The Four Marys

30 Girl I Left Behind Me

32 Has Sorrow Thy Young Days Shaded?

34 I Know My Love

44 I Know Where I'm Goin'

36 I'll Tell Me Ma

38 Johnny, I Hardly Knew Ye

40 The Jolly Beggarman

42 Jug of Punch

45 Kathleen Mavourneen

48 Kerry Dance

58 Lanigan's Ball

50 Loch Lomond

52 Minstrel Boy

54 Molly Bawn

56 Mother Machree

61 The Mountains of Mourne

64 My Wild Irish Rose

66 The Parting Glass

68 The Rose of Tralee

70 She Moved Through the Fair

72 The Skye Boat Song

74 'Tis the Last Rose of Summer

76 Too-Ra-Loo-Ra-Loo-Ral

78 The Wearing of the Green

80 When Irish Eyes Are Smiling

86 Where the River Shannon Flows

82 Whiskey in the Jar

84 Wind That Shakes the Barley

The Ash Grove

Old Welsh Air

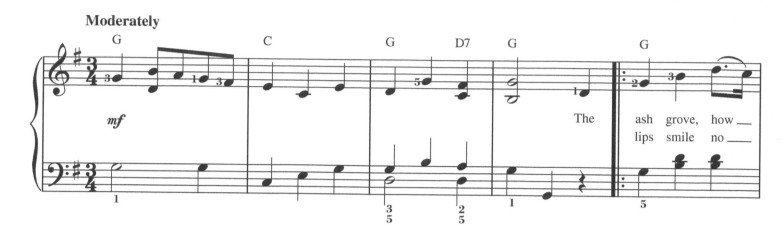

The ash grove, how __
lips smile no __

grace - ful, how plain - ly ___ 'tis ___ speak - ing; the harp through ___ it ___
more, my heart los - es ___ its ___ light - ness; no dream of ___ the ___

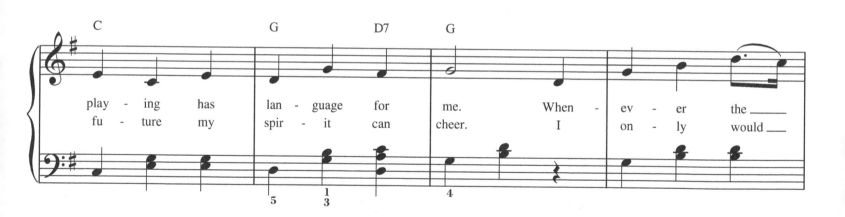

play - ing has lan - guage for me. When - ev - er the ___
fu - ture my spir - it for can cheer. I on - ly would ___

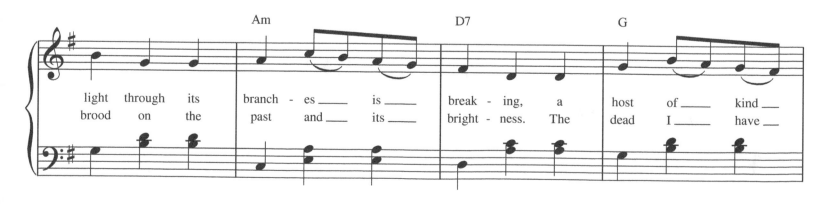

light through its branch - es ___ is ___ break - ing, a host of ___ kind ___
brood on the past and ___ its ___ bright - ness. The dead I ___ have ___

Believe Me, If All Those
Endearing Young Charms

Words and Music by
Thomas Moore

Be - lieve me, if all those en - dear - ing young charms, which I
not _____ while beau - ty and youth are thine own, and thy

gaze on so fond - ly to - day, _____ were to change by to - mor - row, and
cheeks un - pro - faned by a tear, _____ that the fer - vor and faith of a

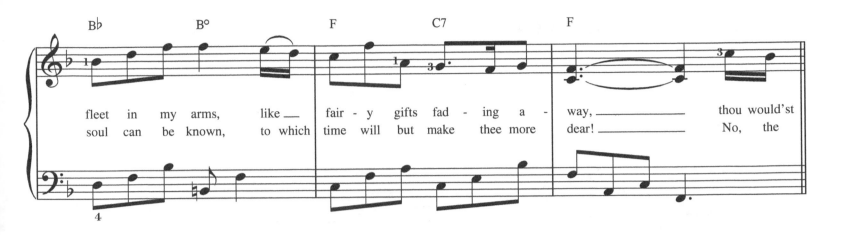

fleet in my arms, like __ fair - y gifts fad - ing a - way, _____ thou would'st
soul can be known, to which time will but make thee more dear! _____ No, the

still be a - dored as this mo - ment thou art let thy love - li - ness fade as it
heart that has tru - ly loved nev - er for - gets let but as tru - ly loves on to the

will; _____ and a - round the dear ru - in, each wish of my heart would en -
close; _____ as a sun - flow - er turns on her god, when he sets, the same

twine it - self ver - dant - ly   still. _____ It is
look which she turned when he

1.

rose. _____

2.

The Bluebells of Scotland

Traditional

Moderately

Oh,	where,	tell	me	where,	is	your ___
	where,	tell	me	where,	did	your ___
	what,	tell	me	what,	does	your ___

High - land	lad - die	gone?	Oh,	where,	tell	me
High - land	lad - die	dwell?	Oh,	where,	tell	me
High - land	lad - die	wear?	Oh,	what,	tell	me

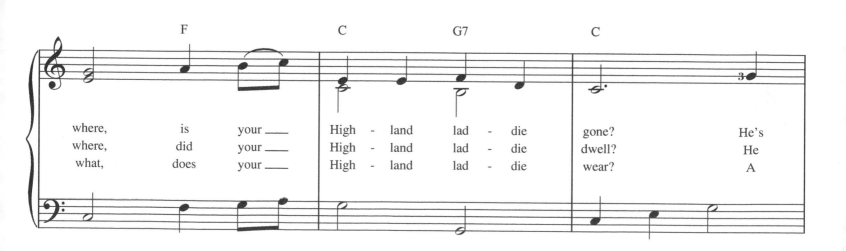

where,	is	your ___	High - land	lad - die	gone?	He's
where,	did	your ___	High - land	lad - die	dwell?	He
what,	does	your ___	High - land	lad - die	wear?	A

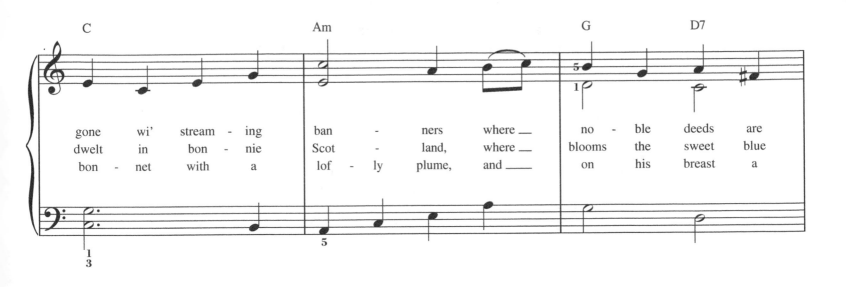

gone wi' stream - ing ban - ners where __ no - ble deeds are
dwelt in bon - nie Scot - land, where __ blooms the sweet blue
bon - net with a lof - ly plume, and __ on his sweet breast a

done. And it's, oh, in my heart I _____
bell. And it's, oh, in my heart I _____
plaid. And it's, oh, in my heart I _____

wish him safe at home. Oh, lad.
lo'e my lad - die well. Oh,
lo'e my High - land

9

A Bunch of Thyme

Traditional Irish Folk Song

Come all you maid - ens young and
thyme, it is a pre - cious
Once, I had a bunch of

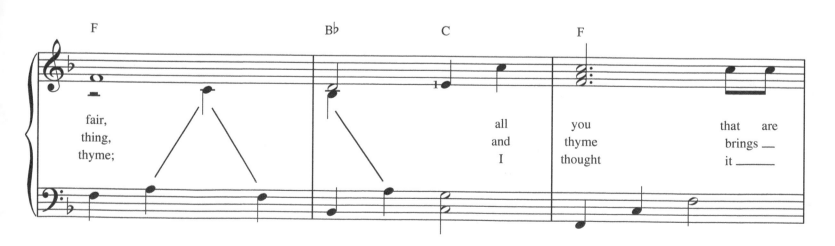

fair, all you that are
thing, and thyme brings —
thyme; I thought it ____

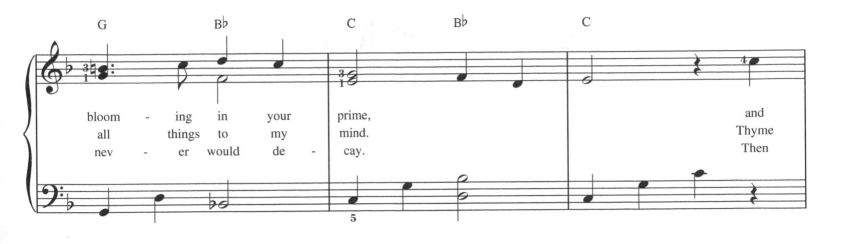

bloom - ing in your prime,
all things to my mind.
nev - er would de - cay.

and
Thyme
Then

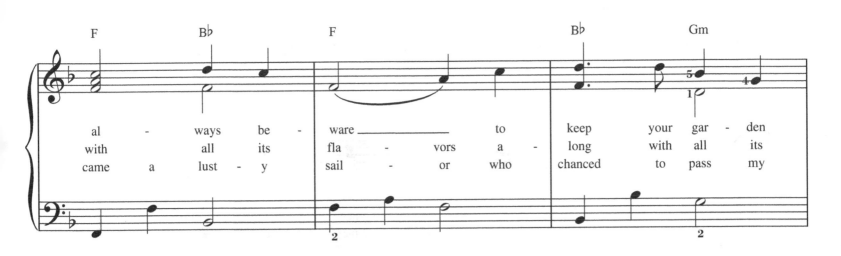

al - ways be - ware _____ to keep your gar - den
with all its fla - vors a - long with all its
came a lust - y sail - or who chanced to pass my

fair; _____ let no man steal a - way your
joys, _____ thyme brings all things to my
way _____ and stole my bunch of thyme a -

thyme.
mind.
way.

For

Cockles and Mussels

(Molly Malone)

Traditional Irish Folk Song

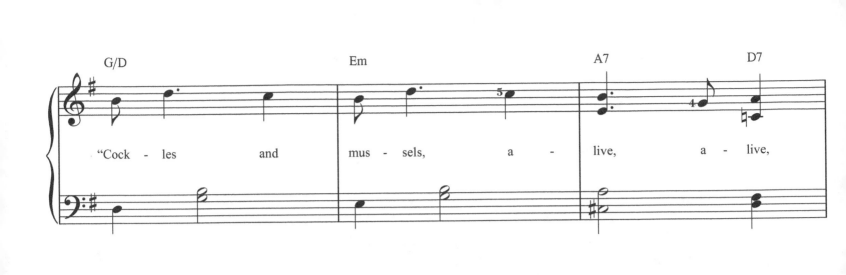

"Cock - les and mus - sels, a - live, a - live,

oh! A - live, a - live, oh! ___ A - live, a - live,

oh!" ___ Cry - ing, "Cock - les and mus - sels, a -

live, a - live, oh." { She { She

oh!" ___

13

The Croppy Boy

Eighteenth Century Irish Folk Song

Moderately

'Twas ear - ly, ear - - ly
ear - ly, ear - - ly
in the guard - house where

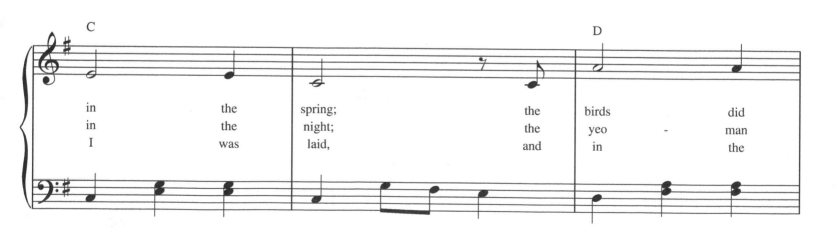

in the spring;
in the night;
I was laid,
the birds did
the yeo - man
and in the

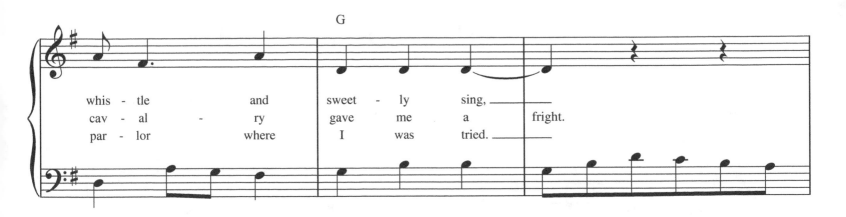

whis - tle and sweet - ly sing,_____
cav - al - ry gave me a fright._____
par - lor where I was tried._____

chang - ing their notes from tree to tree,_____
The yeo - man cav - al - ry was my down -
My sen - tence passed and my cour - age low,_____

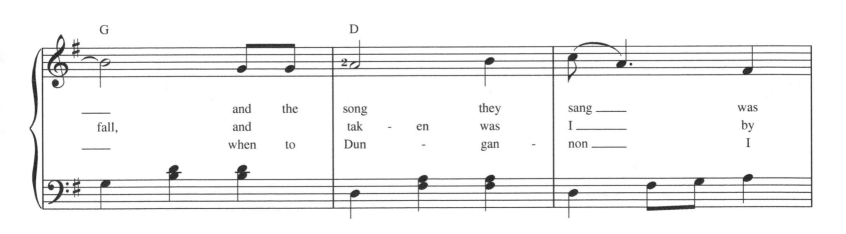

_____ and the song they sang _____ was
fall, and the tak - en was I _____ by
_____ when to Dun - gan - non _____ I

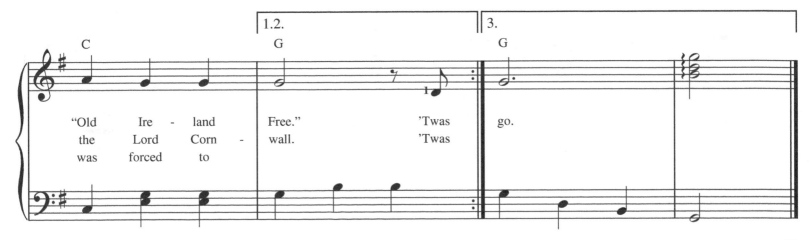

"Old Ire - land Free." 'Twas go.
the Lord Corn - wall. 'Twas
was forced to

15

Danny Boy

(Londonderry Air)

Words by
Frederick Edward Weatherly

Traditional Irish Folk Melody

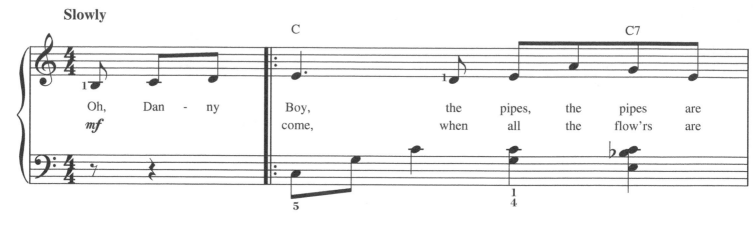

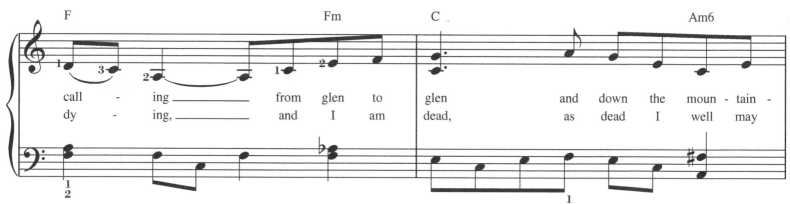

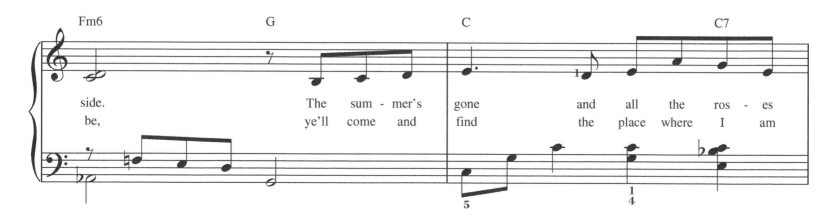

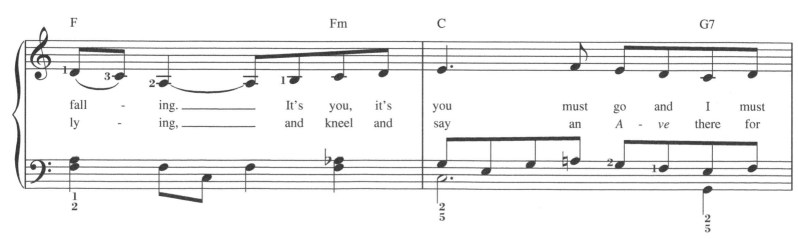

17

Carrickfergus

Traditional Irish Folk Song

Moderately

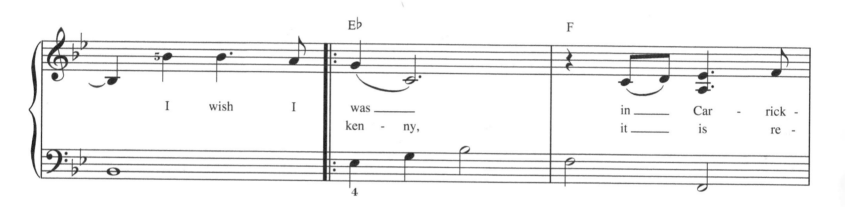

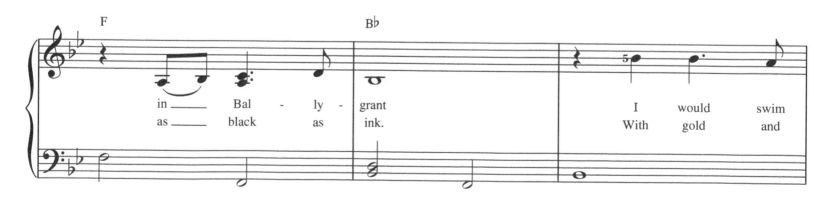

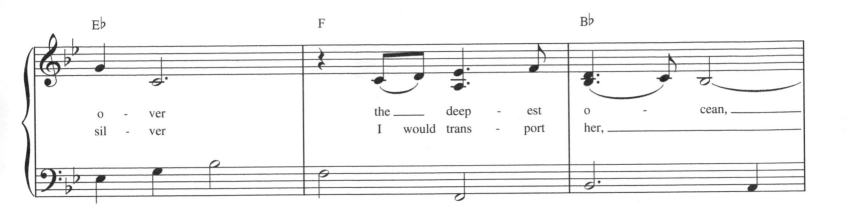

o - ver / sil - ver | the _____ deep - est / I would trans - port | o - _____ cean, _____ / her, _____

_____ / _____ | on - ly for / but I'll sing | nights _____ / no more | in _____ Bal - ly - / now till I get a

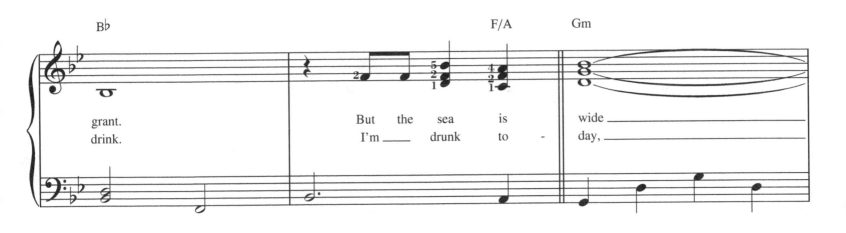

grant. / drink. | But the sea is / I'm _____ drunk to - | wide _____ / day, _____

_____ and I can't swim / but then, I'm sel - | o - ver, _____ / dom so - ber, _____ | nor have _____ / a hand - some

I _____ the _____ wings to fly.
rov - er _____ from ___ town to town.

If I could find me
Ah, but I'm sick now,
a _____ hand - some
my _____ days are

boats - man _____ to fer - ry me o - ver
o - ver. _____ Come, all ye young lads, _____

to my love and die.
and ___ lay me down.

1.
Now, in Kil -

2.

20

Eileen Oge

Words by
Percy French

Music by
Houston Collisson

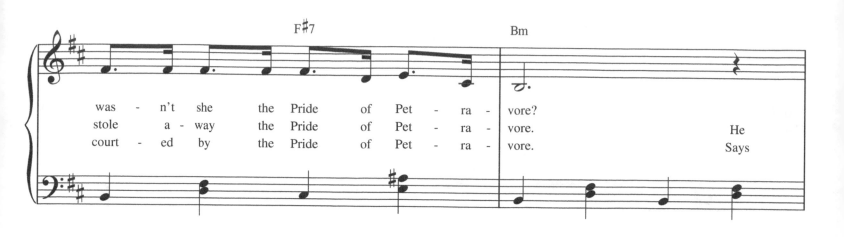

F#7   Bm

was - n't she the Pride of Pet - ra - vore?
stole a - way the Pride of Pet - ra - vore.   He
court - ed by the Pride of Pet - ra - vore.   Says

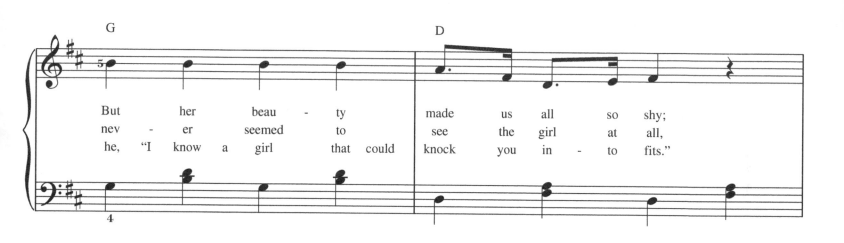

G   D

But her beau - ty made us all so shy;
nev - er seemed to see the girl at all,
he, "I know a girl that could knock you in - to fits."

F#7   Bm

not a man could look her in the eye.
e - ven when she o - gled him un - der - neath her shawl.
At that, Ei - leen near - ly lost her wits.   The

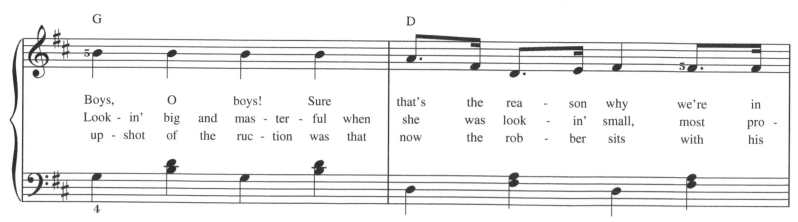

G   D

Boys, O boys! Sure that's the rea - son why we're in
Look - in' big and mas - ter - ful when she was look - in' small, most pro -
up - shot of the ruc - tion was that now the rob - ber sits with his

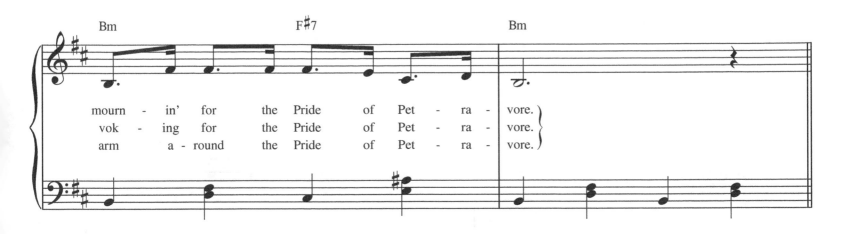

mourn - in' for the Pride of Pet - ra - vore.
vok - ing for the Pride of Pet - ra - vore.
arm a - round the Pride of Pet - ra - vore.

Ei - leen Oge! Me heart is grow - in' grey ev - er since the day you

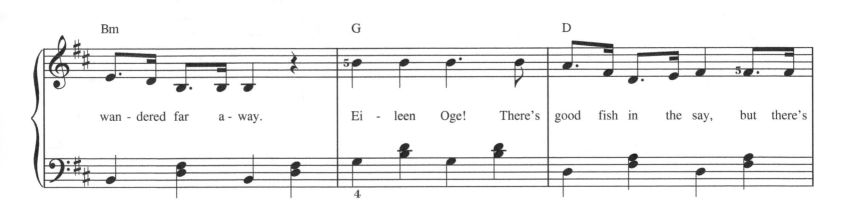

wan - dered far a - way. Ei - leen Oge! There's good fish in the say, but there's

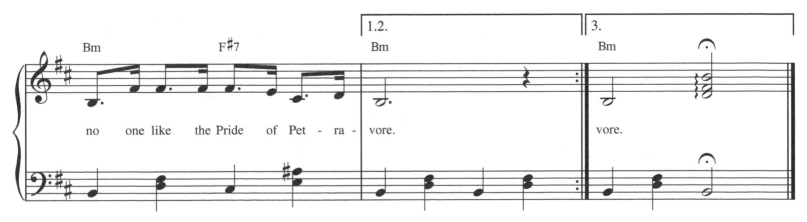

1.2.

no one like the Pride of Pet - ra - vore.

3.

vore.

Finnegan's Wake

Traditional Irish Folk Song

Moderately, in 2

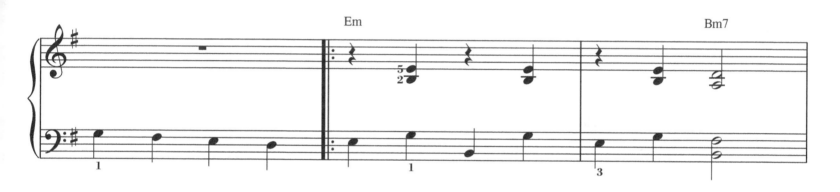

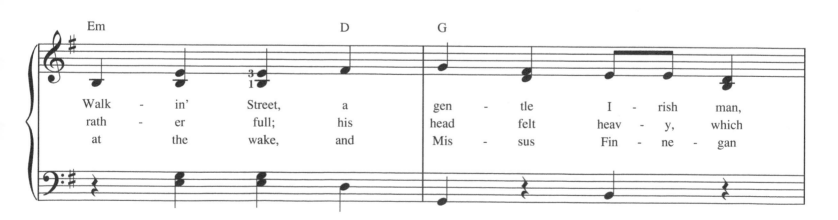

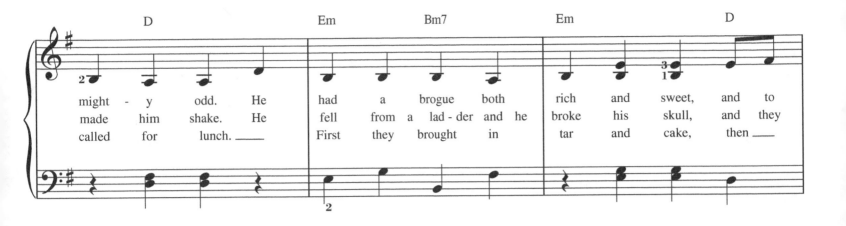

might - y odd. He
made him shake. He
called for lunch. ____

had a brogue both
fell from a lad-der and he
First they brought in

rich and sweet, and to
broke his skull, and they
tar and cake, then ____

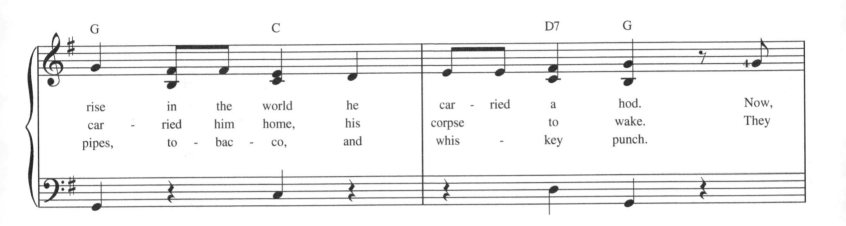

rise in the world he
car - ried him home, his
pipes, to - bac - co, and

car - ried a hod.
corpse to wake.
whis - key punch.

Now,
They

Tim had a sort o' the
rolled him up in a
Bid - dy O' - Bri - en be -

tip - plin' way, with a
nice clean sheet and
gan to cry, "Such a

love for the liq - our poor
laid him out up -
nice clean corpse did you

Tim was born. To
on the bed;
ev - er see? Oh,

help him on with his
To a gal - lon of whis - key
Tim, mav - our - neen, why

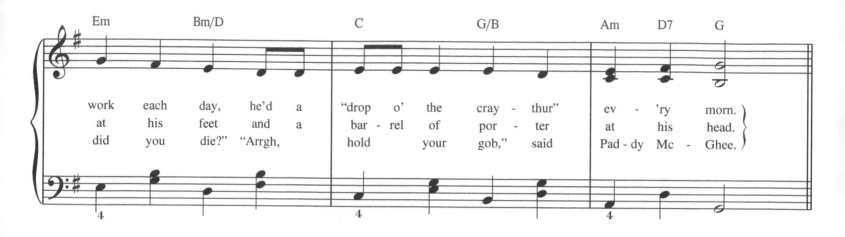

work each day, he'd a "drop o' the cray - thur" ev - 'ry morn.
at his feet and a bar - rel of por - ter at his head.
did you die?" "Arrgh, hold your gob," said Pad - dy Mc - Ghee.

Whack fol the darn, O, dance to your part - ner. Whirl the floor, your

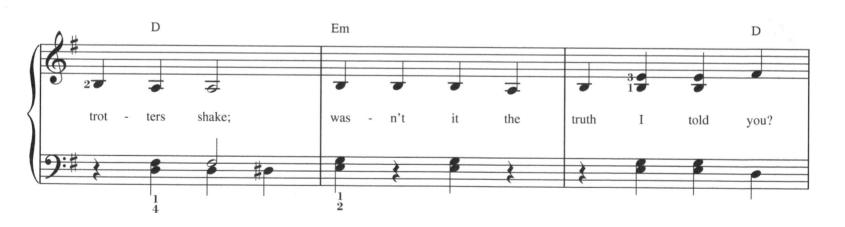

trot - ters shake; was - n't it the truth I told you?

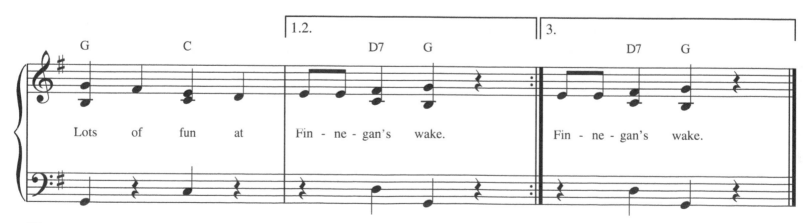

Lots of fun at Fin - ne - gan's wake. Fin - ne - gan's wake.

The Four Marys

Traditional Scottish Song

The Foggy Dew

Traditional Irish Folk Song

Girl I Left Behind Me

Traditional Irish

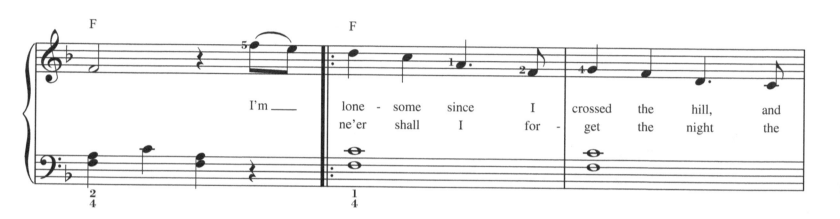

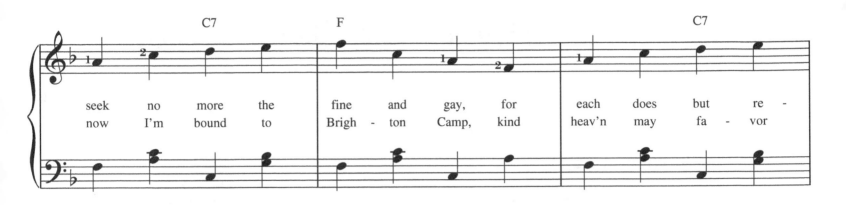

seek no more the / fine and gay, for / each does but re-
now I'm bound to / Brigh - ton Camp, kind / heav'n may fa - vor

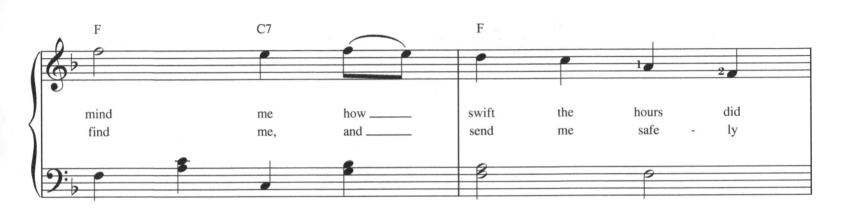

mind / me how ____ / swift the hours did
find / me, and ____ / send me safe - ly

1.

pass a - way with the / girl I left be - / hind me.
back a - gain to the / girl I left be -

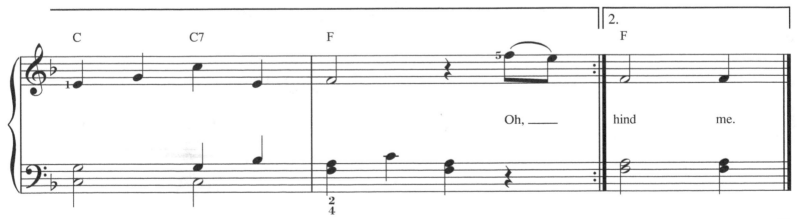

2.

Oh, ____ / hind me.

31

Has Sorrow Thy Young Days Shaded?

Traditional

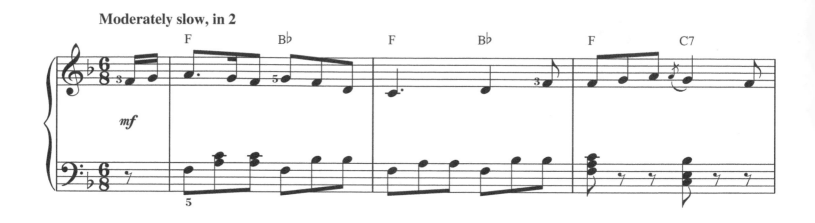

Has — sor - row thy young — days shad - ed, as
love, to that soul — so ten - der, been
hope, like the bird in the sto - ry, that

clouds o'er the morn - ing fleet? _____ Too — fast have those young — days
like our La - ge - nian mine, _____ where _ spar - kles of gold - en
flit - ed from tree to tree _____ with the tal - is - man's glit - ter - ing

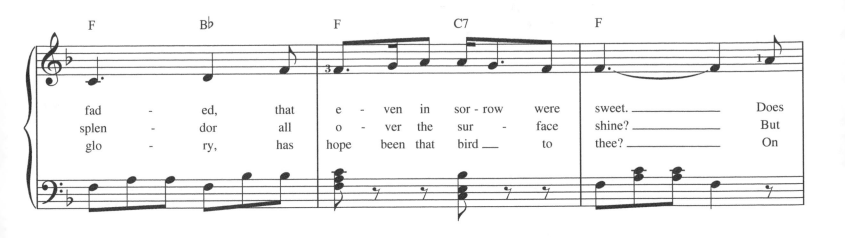

fad - ed, that | e - ven in sor - row were | sweet. _____ Does
splen - dor all | o - ver the sur - face | shine? _____ But
glo - ry, has | hope been that bird __ to | thee? _____ On

Time with his cold __ wing | with - er, each | feel - ing that once __ was
if in pur - suit we go | deep - er, al | lured by the gleam __ that
branch af - ter branch __ a - | light - ing, the | gem did she still __ dis -

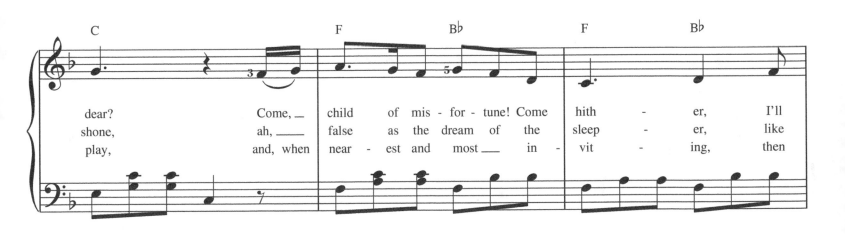

dear? | Come, __ child of mis - for - tune! Come | hith - er, I'll
shone, ah, ____ | false as the dream of the | sleep - er, like
play, | and, when near - est and most __ in - | vit - ing, then

weep with thee, tear for | tear. Has __ | way.
love, the bright ore is | gone. Has __
waft the fair gem a - |

I Know My Love

Traditional Irish Folk Song

still she cried, "I love him the best, and a troubled mind, sure, can

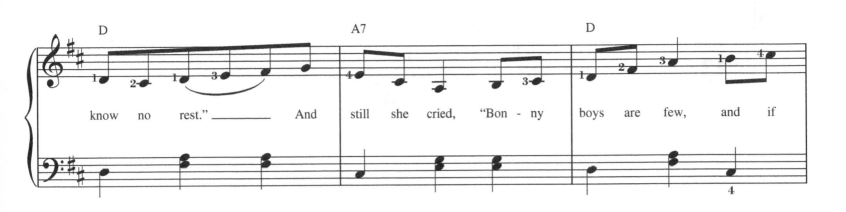

know no rest." _____ And still she cried, "Bon - ny boys are few, and if

my love leaves me, what will I do?"

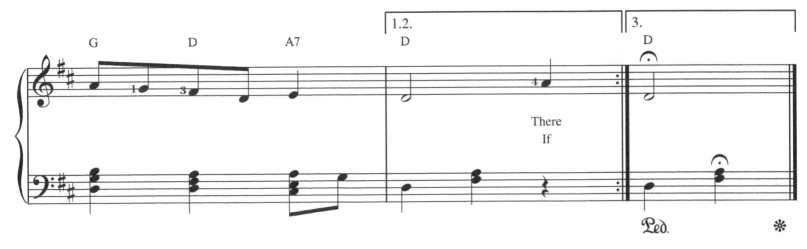

1.2.

There

3.

If

I'll Tell Me Ma

Traditional Irish Folk Song

Moderately fast

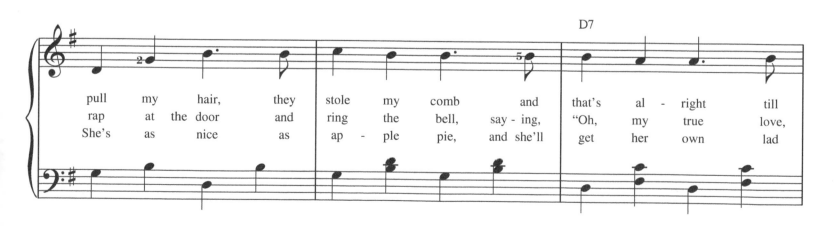

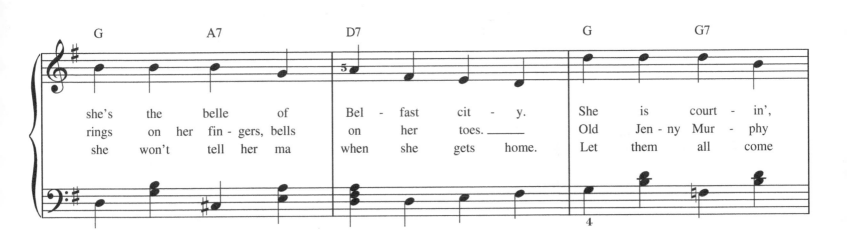

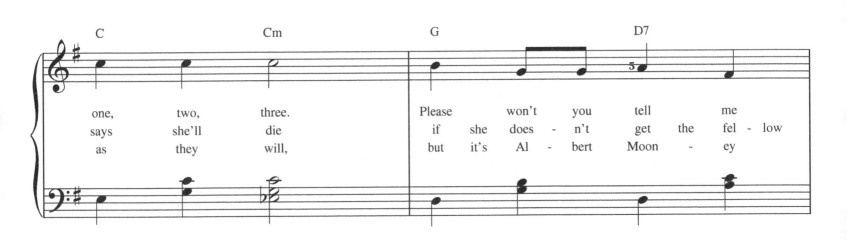

Johnny, I Hardly Knew Ye

Traditional Irish Folk Song

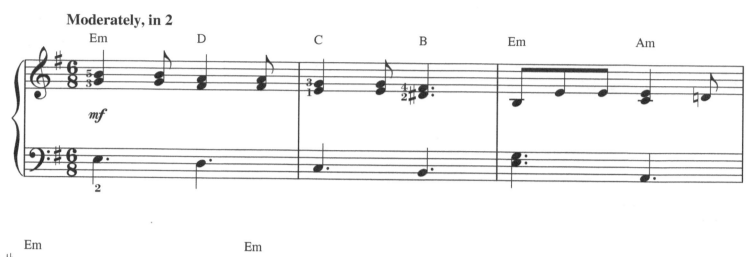

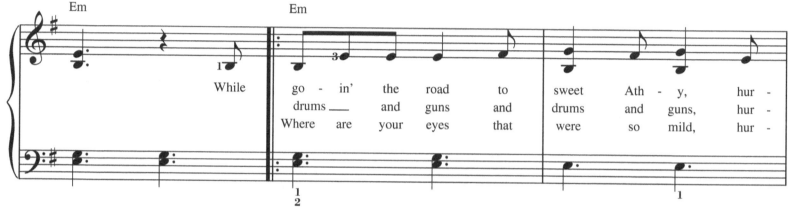

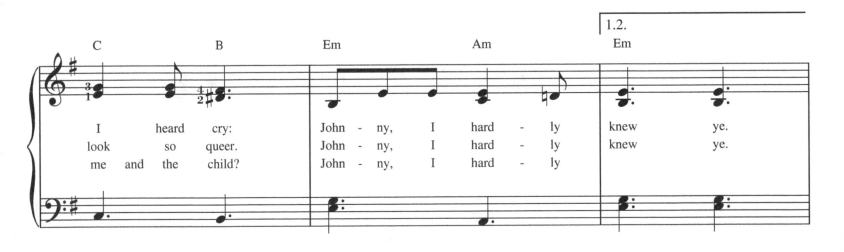

39

The Jolly Beggarman

Traditional Irish Folk Song

Brightly, in 2

It's

of a jol - ly beg - gar - man came trip - ping o'er the
would not lie with - in the barn nor yet with - in the
farm - er's daugh - ter, she got up to bolt the kitch - en

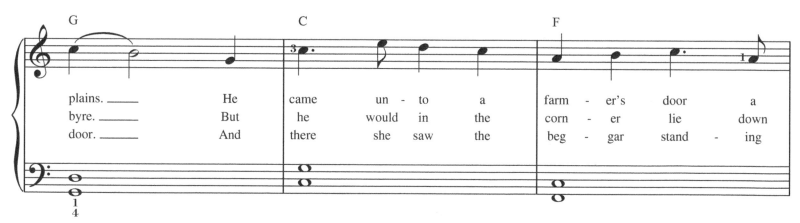

plains. _____ He came un - to a farm - er's door a
byre. _____ But he would in the corn - er lie down
door. _____ And there she saw the beg - gar stand - ing

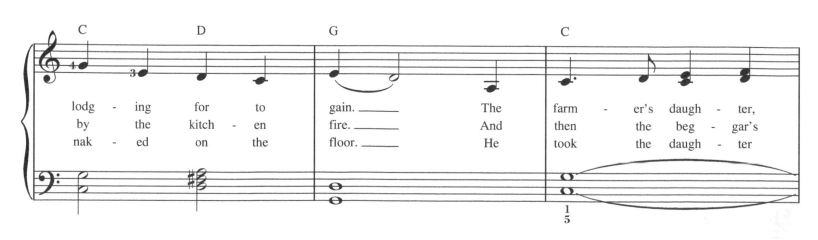

lodg - ing for to gain. _____ The farm - er's daugh - ter,
by the kitch - en fire. _____ And then the beg - gar's
nak - ed on the floor. _____ He took the daugh - ter

Jug of Punch

Ulster Folk Song

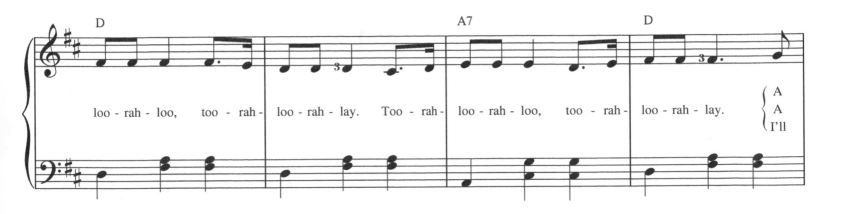

loo - rah - loo, too - rah - loo - rah - lay. Too - rah - loo - rah - loo, too - rah - loo - rah - lay.

A
A
I'll

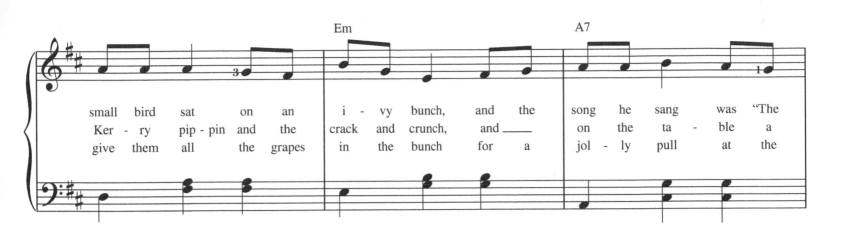

small bird sat on an i - vy bunch, and the song he sang was "The
Ker - ry pip - pin and the crack and crunch, and ___ on the ta - ble a
give them all the grapes in the bunch for a jol - ly pull at the

1.2.

Jug of Punch."
jug of punch.

What more di - y jug of punch.
All ye

3.

I Know Where I'm Goin'

English Folksong

Kathleen Mavourneen

Words and Music by
Frederick N. Crouch

Kath - leen Ma -
Kath - leen Ma -

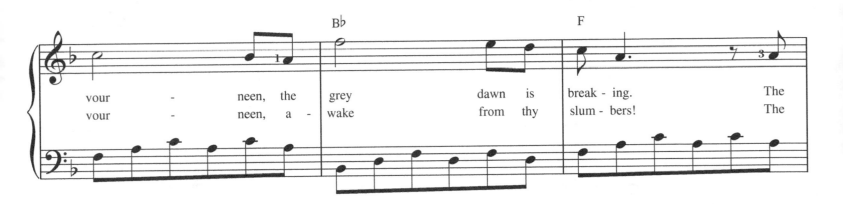

vour - neen, the grey dawn is break - ing. The
vour - neen, a - wake from thy slum - bers! The

horn of the hunt - er is ____ heard ____ on the
blue moun - tains flow in the ____ sun's ____ gold - en

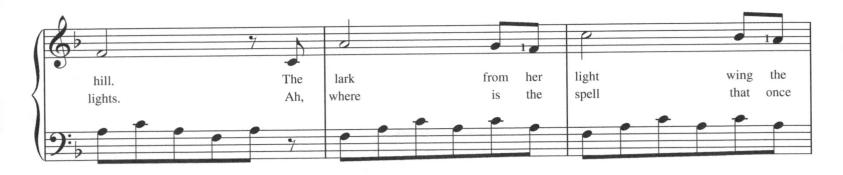

hill. The lark from her light wing the
lights. Ah, where is the spell that once

years, and it may be for - ev - er. Then ___

why _____ art thou si - lent, thou, voice of my

heart? It may _____ be for years, and it

may be for - ev - er. Then why _____ art thou si - lent,

Kath - leen Ma - vour - neen?

vour - neen?

Kerry Dance

By J.L. Molloy

Moderately, in 2

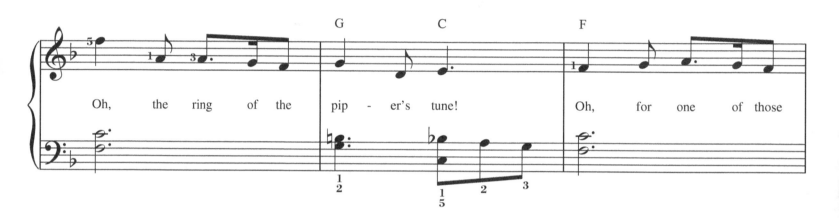

Loch Lomond

Scottish Folk Song

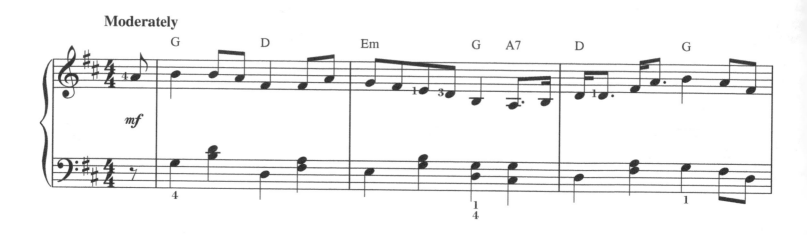

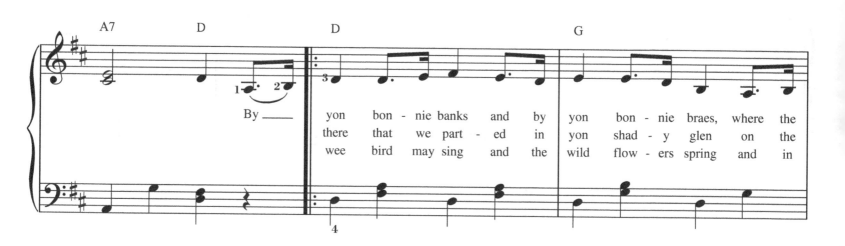

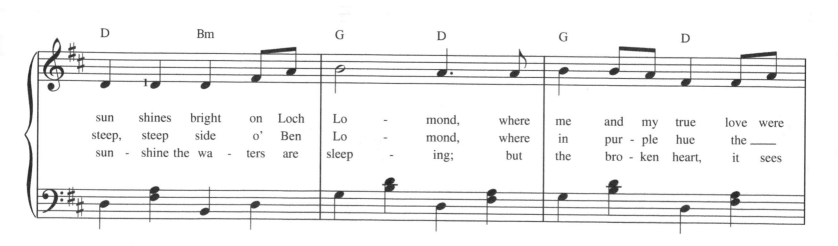

ev-er want to gae on the bon-nie, bon-nie banks o' Loch Lo - mond.
High-land hills we view, and the morn shines out frae the gloam - ing. } Oh, ___
nae ___ sec-ond spring, and the world does nae ken how we're greet - ing.

ye'll take the high road and I'll take the low road, and I'll be in Scot-land a -

fore ye. But me an' my true love will nev - er meet a - gain on the

bon - nie, bon - nie banks o' Loch Lo - mond. { 'Twas ___ / The ___ Lo - mond.

Minstrel Boy

Traditional

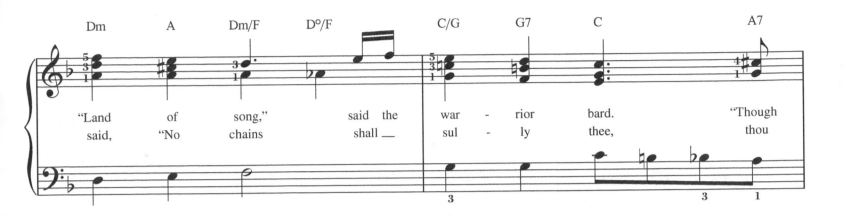

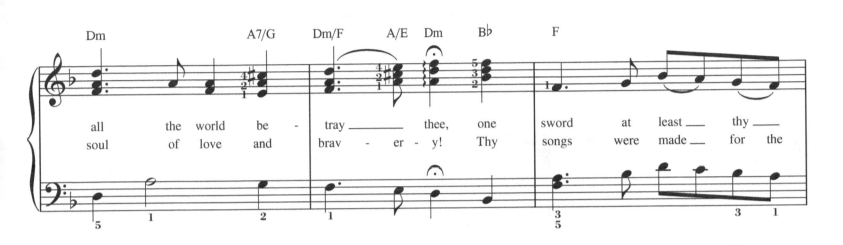

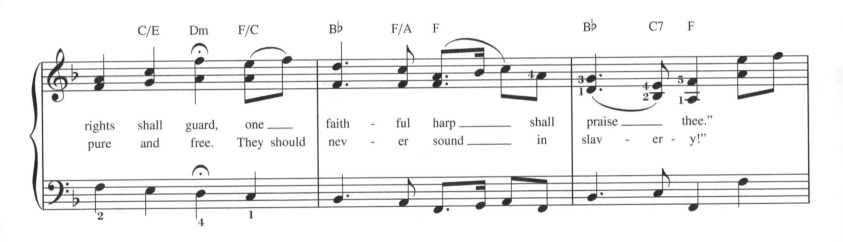

53

Molly Bawn

Words and Music by
Samuel Lover

Oh! Mol- ly Bawn, why leave me
pret- ty flow'rs were made to

pin- ing, all lone- ly wait- ing here for you? While the
bloom, dear, all the pret- ty stars were made to shine, and the

stars a- bove are bright- ly shin- ing be- cause they've noth- ing else to
pret- ty girls were made for boys, dear, and may- be you were made for

do. The flow- ers late were o- pen keep- ing, to
mine. The wick- ed watch- dog here is snarl- ing. He

try a ri - val blush with you, but their moth - er, Na - ture, set them
takes me for a thief, you see, for he knows I'd steal you, Mol - ly,

sleep - ing, with their ros - y fac - es washed with dew.)
dar - lin', and _____ then trans - port - ed I should be.) Oh!

Mol - ly Bawn, why leave me pin - ing, all lone - ly wait - ing here for you? The _____

stars a - bove are bright - ly shin - ing be - cause they've noth - ing else to

do. _____ Mol - ly Bawn, _____ Mol - ly Bawn! Now the Bawn!

Mother Machree

Words by
Rida Johnson Young

Music by
Chauncey Olcott and Ernest R. Ball

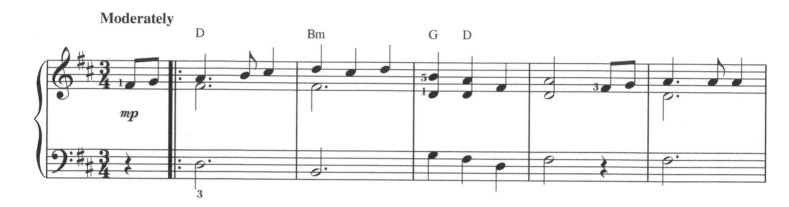

There's a   spot   in my   heart which   no
Ev - 'ry   sor - row or   care   in   the

col - leen   may   own.   There's   a   depth   in my   soul   nev - er
dear   days   gone   by   was   made   bright   by   the   light   of   the

sound - ed   or   known.   There's   a   place   in my   mem - 'ry,   my
smile   in   your   eye.   Like   a   can - dle   that's   set   in   a

Lanigan's Ball

Traditional Irish Folk Song

Moderately fast, in 2

In the town of A - thol lived one
it was me - self had free
boys were all mer - ry, the

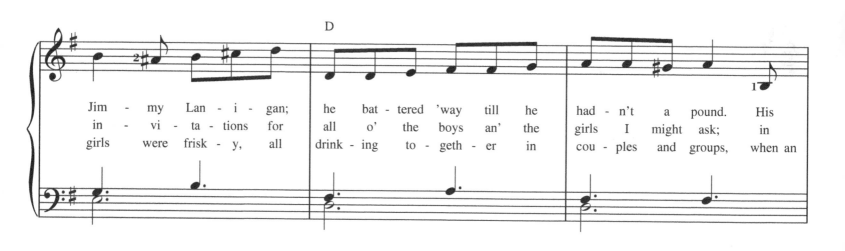

Jim - my Lan - i - gan; he bat - tered 'way till he had - n't a pound. His
in - vi - ta - tions for all o' the boys an' the girls I might ask; in
girls were frisk - y, all drink - ing to - geth - er in cou - ples and groups, when an

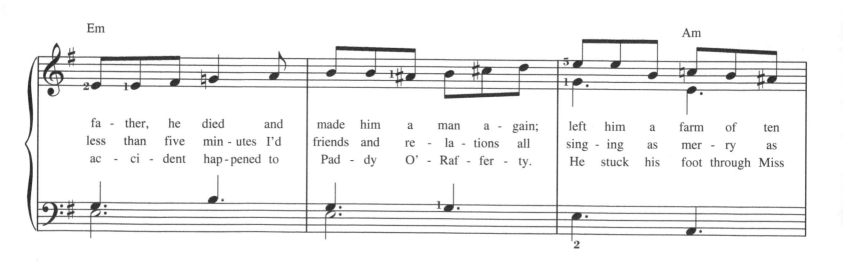

fa - ther, he died and made him a man a - gain; left him a farm of ten
less than five min - utes I'd friends and re - la - tions all sing - ing as mer - ry as
ac - ci - dent hap - pened to Pad - dy O' - Raf - fer - ty. He stuck his foot through Miss

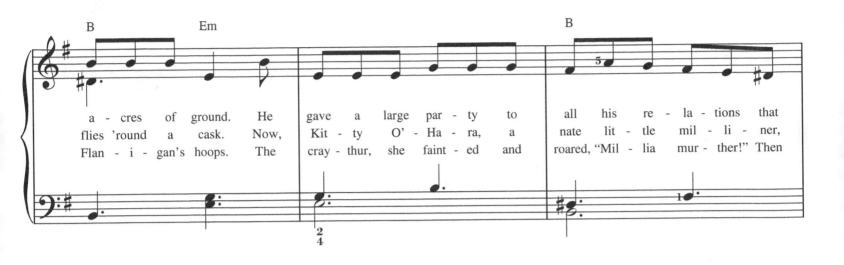

a - cres of ground. He gave a large par - ty to all his re - la - tions that
flies 'round a cask. Now, Kit - ty O' - Ha - ra, a nate lit - tle mil - li - ner,
Flan - i - gan's hoops. The cray - thur, she faint - ed and roared, "Mil - lia mur - ther!" Then

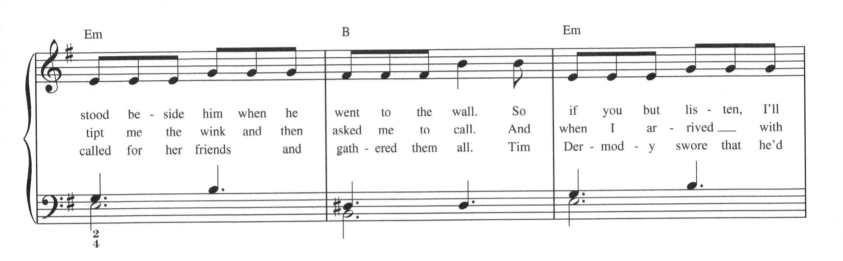

stood be - side him when he went to the wall. So if you but lis - ten, I'll
tipt me the wink and then asked me to call. And when I ar - rived ___ with
called for her friends and gath - ered them all. And Tim Der - mod - y swore that he'd

make your eyes glis - ten with the rows and the 'rup - tions at Lan - i - gan's Ball.
Tim - o - thy Gal - li - gan, just in time for Lan - i - gan's Ball.
go ___ no fur - ther, but have sat - is - fac - tion at Lan - i - gan's Ball!

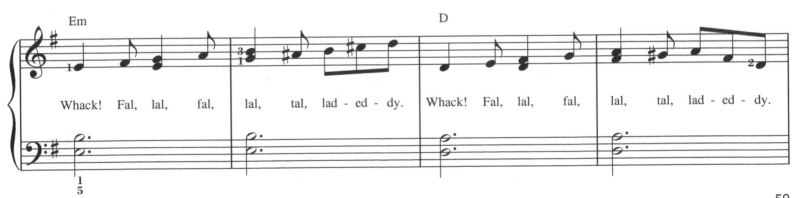

Whack! Fal, lal, fal, lal, tal, lad - ed - dy. Whack! Fal, lal, fal, lal, tal, lad - ed - dy.

The Mountains of Mourne

Words by
Percy French

Traditional Irish Melody

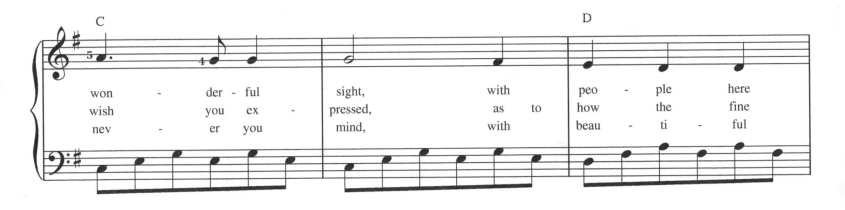

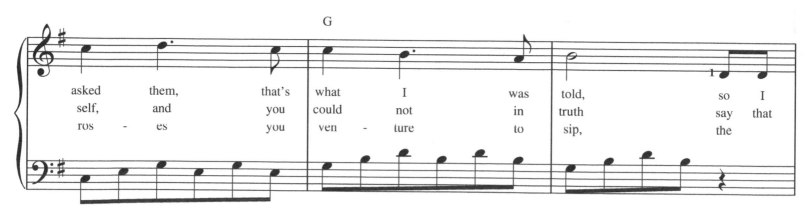

My Wild Irish Rose

Words and Music by
Chauncey Olcott

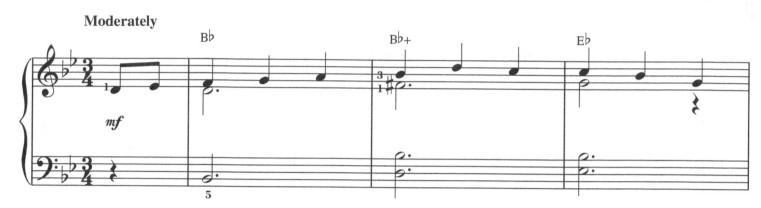

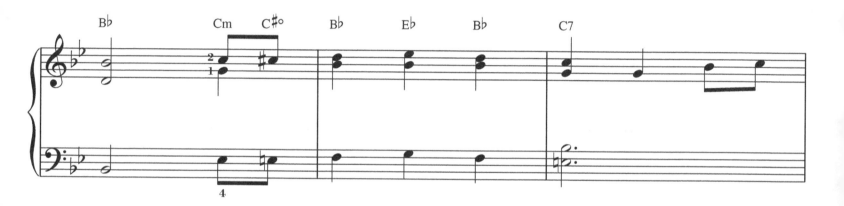

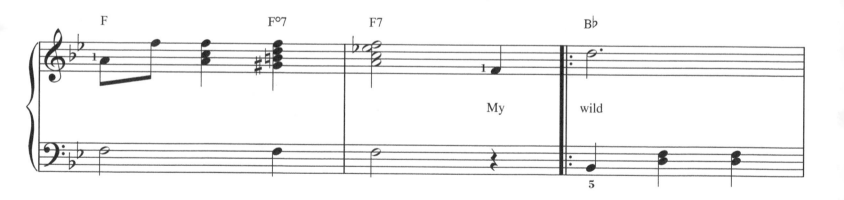

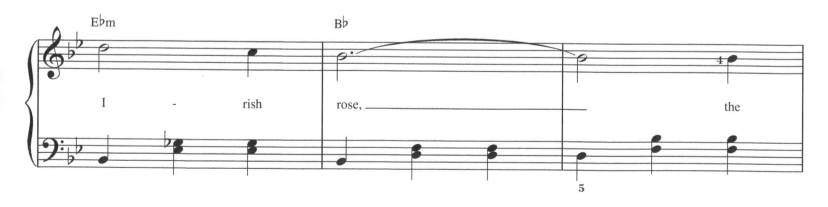

The Parting Glass

Irish Folksong

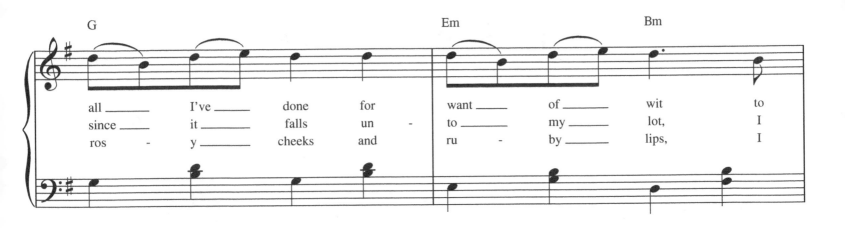

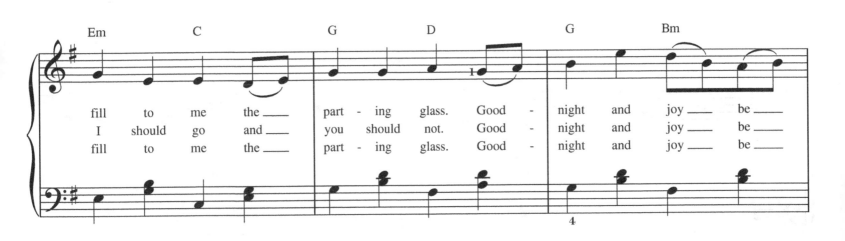

The Rose of Tralee

Words by
C. Mordaunt Spencer

Music by
Charles W. Glover

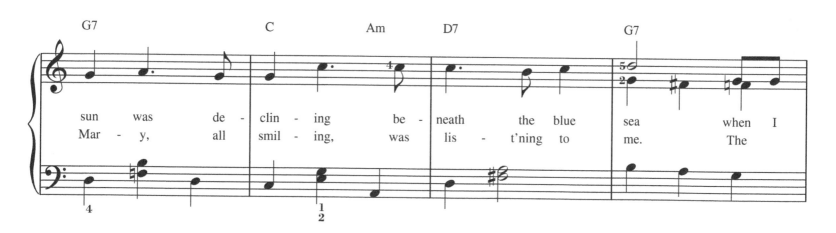

stands in the beau - ti - ful vale of Tra - lee. She was
I won the heart of the rose of Tra - lee. Though

love - ly and fair as the rose of ___ the ___ sum - mer, yet 'twas not her

beau - ty a - lone that won me. Oh, no! 'Twas the truth in her

rit.   *a tempo*

eye ev - er dawn - ing that made me love Mar - y, the rose of Tra -

lee. The

She Moved Through the Fair

Traditional Irish Melody

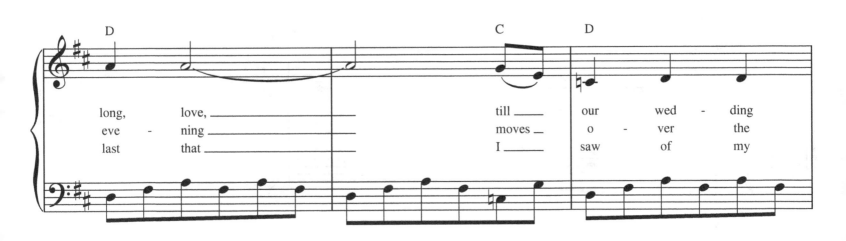

71

The Skye Boat Song

Traditional

Moderately slow, in 2

Last time to Coda

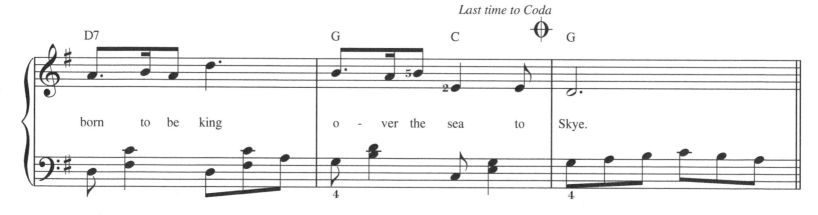

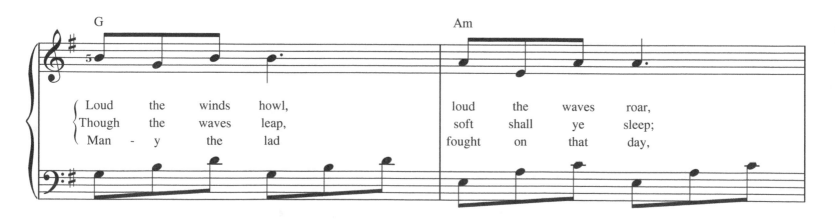

thun - der - claps rend the air.
o - cean's a roy - al bed.
well the clay - more could wield.

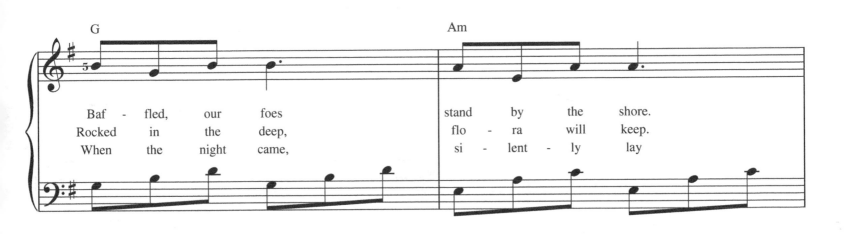

Baf - fled, our foes stand by the shore.
Rocked in the deep, flo - ra will keep.
When the night came, si - lent - ly lay

1.2.

Fol - low, they will not dare.
Watch by your wea - ry head.
dead on Cul - lo - den's

3.

field.

D.C. al Coda

Coda

Skye.

73

'Tis the Last Rose of Summer

Words by
Thomas Moore

Music by
Richard Alfred Milliken

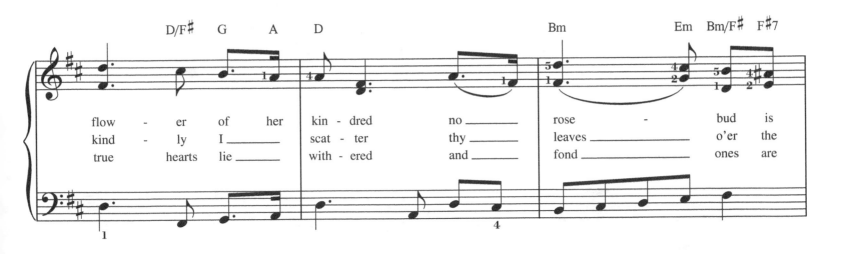

flow - er of her kin - dred no _____ rose - bud is
kind - ly I _____ scat - ter thy _____ leaves _____ o'er the
true hearts lie _____ with - ered and _____ fond _____ ones are

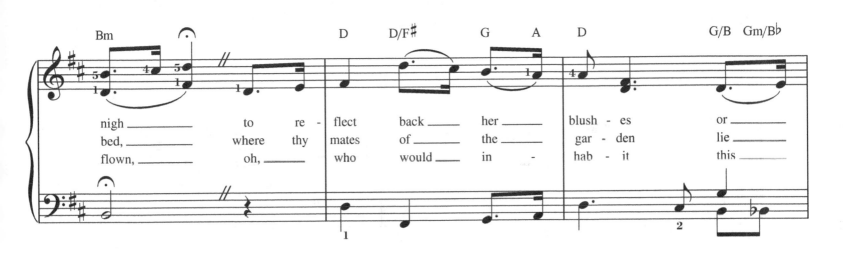

nigh _____ to re - flect back _____ her _____ blush - es or _____
bed, _____ where thy mates of _____ the _____ gar - den lie _____
flown, _____ oh, _____ who would _____ in - hab - it this _____

give _____ sigh for sigh.
scent - less and _____ dead.
bleak ___ world a - lone?

1.2.
I'll _____
So, _____

3.
rit.

75

Too-Ra-Loo-Ra-Loo-Ral

(That's an Irish Lullaby)

Words and Music by
James R. Shannon

O - ver in Kil - lar - ney, _____ man - y years a - go, _____ me
Oft, in dreams, I wan - der _____ to that cot a - gain. _____ I

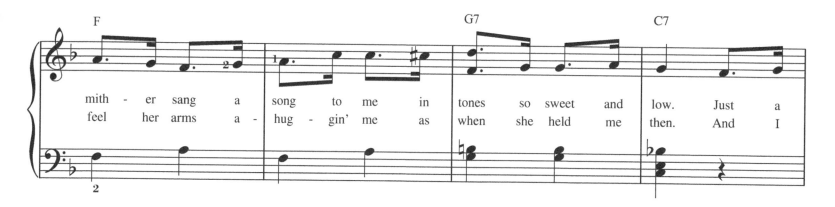

mith - er sang a song to me in tones so sweet and low. Just a
feel her arms a - hug - gin' me as when she held me then. And I

sim - ple lit - tle dit - ty, in her good ould I - rish way, and I'd
hear her voice a - hum - min' to me as in days of yore, and when she

The Wearing of the Green

Eighteenth Century Irish Folk Song

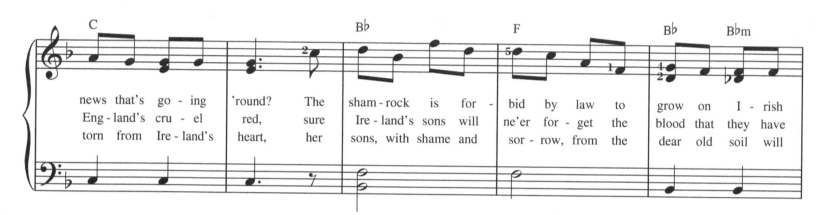

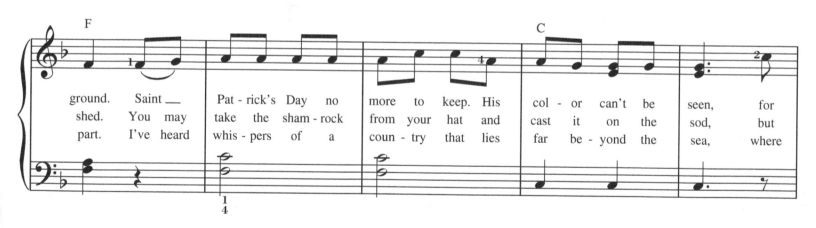

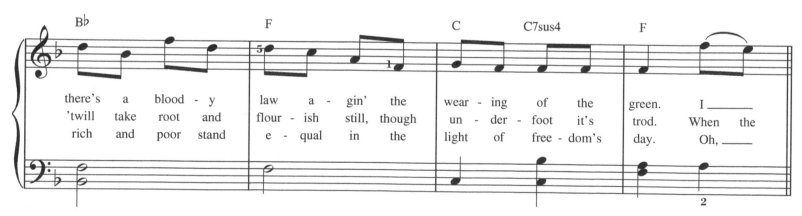

met with Nap - per | Tand - y and he | took me by the | hand, and he
law can stop the | blades of grass from | grow - ing as they | grow, and _____
Er - in, must we | leave you, driv - en | by the ty - rant's | hand? Must we

said, "How's poor old | Ire - land and | how _____ does she | stand? She's the
when the leaves in | sum - mer - time their | ver - dure dare not | show, then _____
ask a moth - er's | wel - come from a | strange but hap - pier | land? Where the

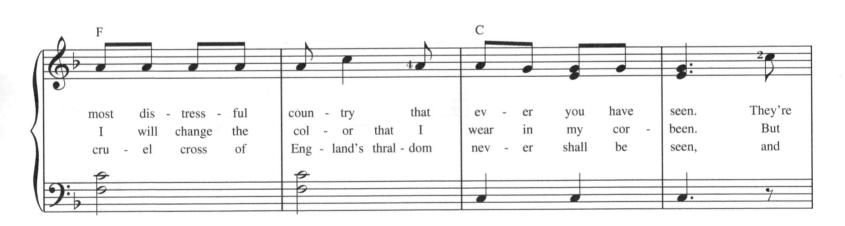

most dis - tress - ful | coun - try that | ev - er you have | seen. They're
I will change the | col - or that I | wear in my cor - | been. But
cru - el cross of | Eng - land's thral - dom | nev - er shall be | seen, and

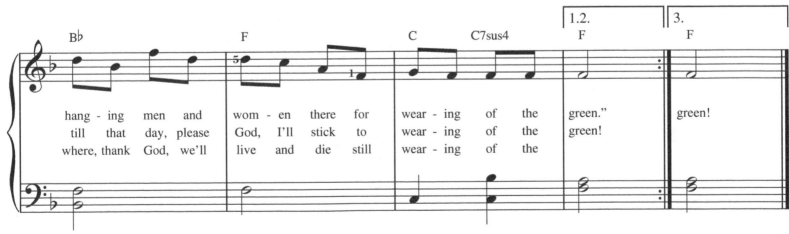

hang - ing men and | wom - en there for | wear - ing of the | green." | green!
till that day, please | God, I'll stick to | wear - ing of the | green!
where, thank God, we'll | live and die still | wear - ing of the

When Irish Eyes Are Smiling

Words by
Chauncey Olcott and George Graff, Jr.

Music by
Ernest R. Ball

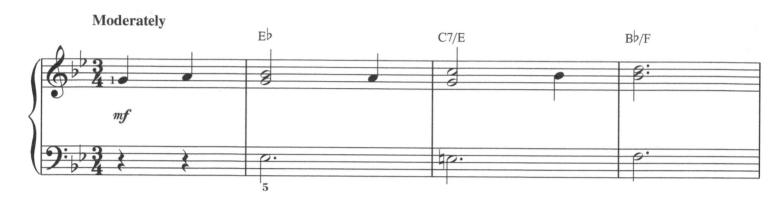

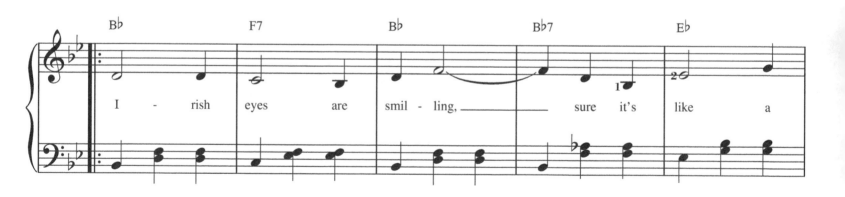

Whiskey in the Jar

Traditional Irish Folk Song

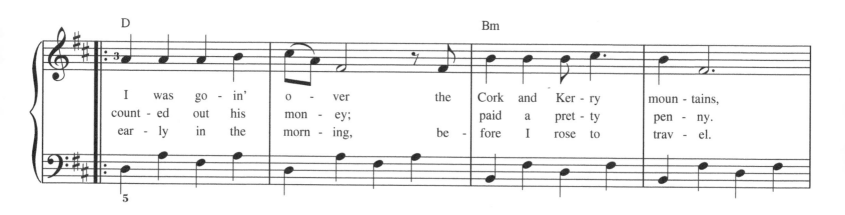

I was go - in' o - ver the Cork and Ker - ry moun - tains,
count - ed out his mon - ey; paid a pret - ty pen - ny.
ear - ly in the morn - ing, be - fore I rose to trav - el.

met with Cap - tain Far - rell and his mon - ey he was
Put it in me pock - et and I took it home to
Up rides a band of foot - men and like - wise rash - er

count - in'.
Jen - ny.
Far - rell.

I first pro - duced me pis -
And she sighed and she swore
Well, I drew up - on me pis -

Wind That Shakes the Barley

Words and Music by
Robert Dwyer Joyce

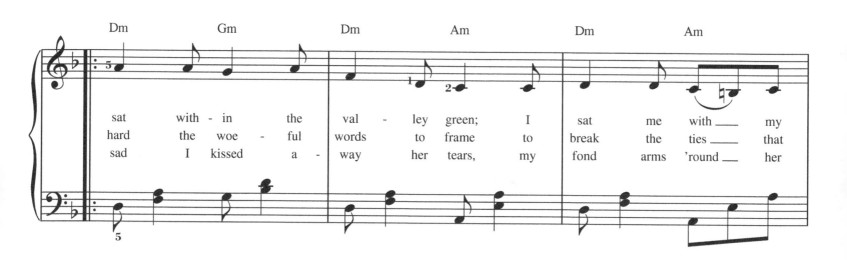

sat with - in the | val - ley green; I | sat me with ___ my
hard the woe - ful | words to frame to | break me the ties ___ that
sad I kissed a - | way her tears, my | fond arms 'round ___ her

true love. _____ My | sad heart strove the | two be - tween, the
bound us. _____ But | hard - er still to | bear the shame of
fling - ing. _____ The | foe - man's shot burst | on our ears from

old   love   and _____ the   new   love. _____   The   old   for   her,   the
for - eign   chains _ a - round   us. _____   And   so   I   said, "The
out   the   wild - wood ring - ing. _____   A   bul - let pierced my

new   that made   me   think   on   Ire - land   dear - ly,   while
moun - tain glen I'll   seek   at   morn - ing   ear - ly,   and
true   love's side   in   life's   young spring so   ear - ly,   and

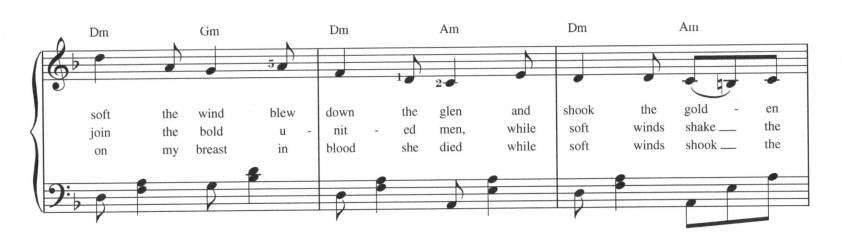

soft   the   wind   blew   down   the   glen   and   shook   the   gold - en
join   the   bold   u - nit - ed men,   while soft   winds shake _ the
on   my   breast   in   blood   she   died   while soft   winds shook _ the

1.2.
bar - ley.   'Twas
bar - ley.   While

3.
bar - ley.

rit.

85

Where the River Shannon Flows

By James J. Russell